SAILING THE SOLAR SYSTEM

THE NEXT 100 YEARS OF SPACE EXPLORATION

by Nel Yomtov

Raintree is an imprint of Capstone Global Library Limited, a company incorporated in England and
Wales having its registered office at 264 Banbury Road, Oxford, OX2 7DY Registered company
number: 6695582

www.raintree.co.uk
myorders@raintree.co.uk

Text © Capstone Global Library Limited 2017
The moral rights of the proprietor have been asserted.

Edited by Mandy Robbins
Art Directed by Nathan Gassman
Designed by Ted Williams
Original illustrations © Capstone Global Library Limited 2017
Illustrated by Alan Brown
Coloured by Giovanni Pota
Picture research by Jo Miller
Production by Katy LaVigne
Originated by Capstone Press
Printed and bound in China

ISBN 978 1 4747 1213 2
20 19 18 17 16
10 9 8 7 6 5 4 3 2 1

British Library Cataloguing in Publication Data
A full catalogue record for this book is available from the British Library.

Acknowledgements
We would like to thank the following for permission to reproduce photographs: Design Element:
Shutterstock: pixelparticle (backgrounds)

CONTENTS

After the war, von Braun and his team joined American scientists to help develop rockets. Meanwhile, the Soviet Union expanded its rocket program, and an intense rivalry developed between the two nations.

The Americans stole a German scientist to compete with the Soviets? Finally, this story's getting good!

"On October 4, 1957, the Soviets launched Sputnik I, *the first artificial satellite. The news shocked and disappointed Americans.*"

"On January 31, 1958, the United States launched its first satellite, Explorer I. *The race into space was in full swing!*"

"In July 1958, President Eisenhower established the National Aeronautics and Space Administration (NASA). He said America's space exploration would be for peaceful and scientific purposes."

It says here the Soviets beat the United States into space again, Luna.

Yep, on April 12, 1961, cosmonaut Yuri Gagarin became the first human sent into space when he orbited Earth.

But it was close. Three weeks later, Alan Shepard became the first American into space.

SALLY RIDE ||||||||||||||

The Soviets sent the first woman, Valentina Tereshkova, into space in 1963. It wasn't until 20 years later that the United States sent the first American woman, Sally Ride, into space. On June 18, 1983, Sally made her historic voyage on the space shuttle *Challenger*. She flew two missions in 1984 and 1986. Sally went on to start her own company to help inspire young women to follow their interests in science and maths.

In 1961, President John F. Kennedy set a bold goal when speaking to a joint session of Congress.

"I believe that this nation should commit itself to achieving the goal, before this decade is out, of landing a man on the Moon and returning him safely to the Earth."

Let me guess: the Soviets beat the United States again?

Not this time! On July 10, 1969, aboard the *Apollo 11* mission, U.S. astronauts Buzz Aldrin and Neil Armstrong became the first humans on the Moon.

SHHHH!

About time.

Eventually, the Americans and the Soviets realised they could accomplish more by working together. In 1975 they launched the joint Apollo-Soyuz project. Spacecraft launched from opposite ends of the Earth met in orbit.

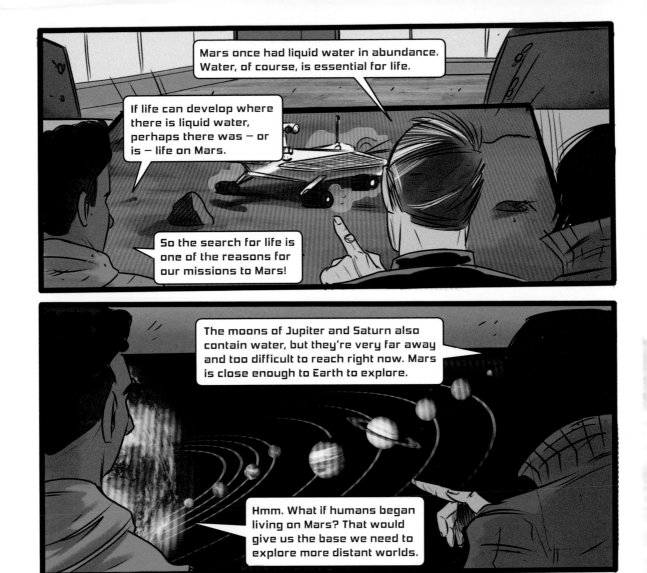

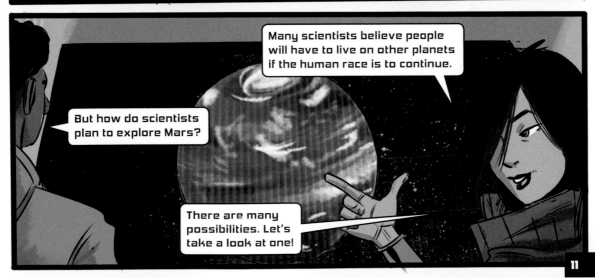

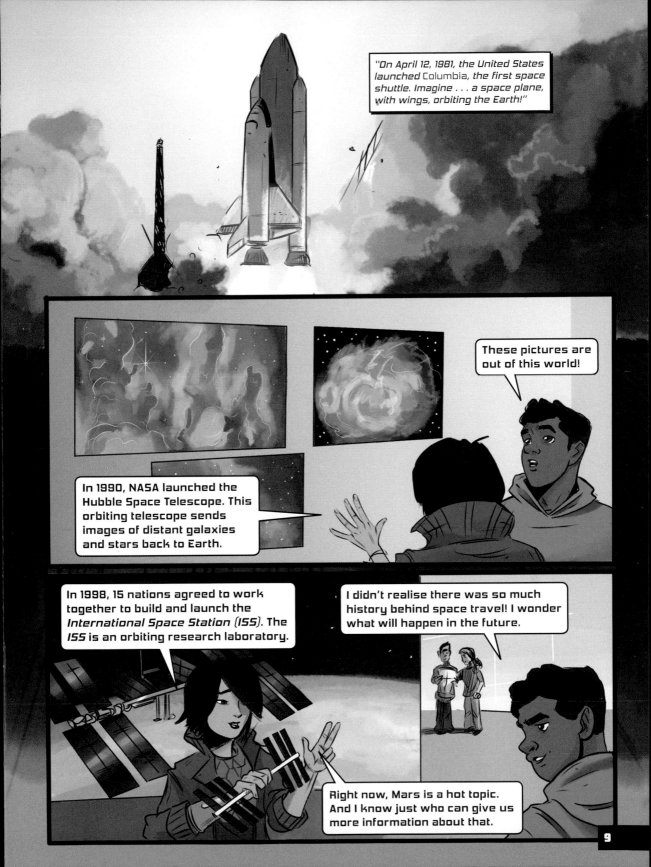

Hi, Luna! What brings you to the museum today?

Hi, Alex. My friend Ron and I want to know what makes Mars so special — and what scientists are hoping to find there.

Nice to meet you, Ron. I can help you with those questions.

Do you remember the Mars *Pathfinder* spacecraft and its rover probe *Sojourner* that NASA landed on Mars in 1997?

Sure! *Pathfinder* landed on Mars' surface and took thousands of photos of the planet. Then it released *Sojourner*, which roamed around analysing the soil and rocks.

The mission was so successful two more rovers were landed on Mars a few years later.

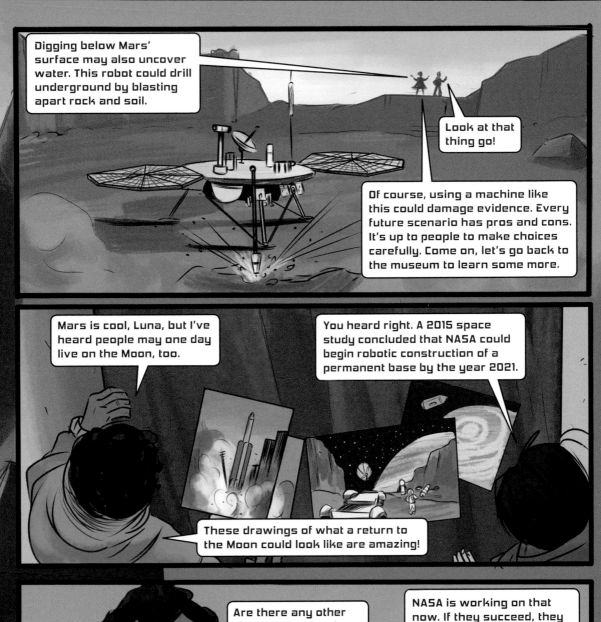

Digging below Mars' surface may also uncover water. This robot could drill underground by blasting apart rock and soil.

Look at that thing go!

Of course, using a machine like this could damage evidence. Every future scenario has pros and cons. It's up to people to make choices carefully. Come on, let's go back to the museum to learn some more.

Mars is cool, Luna, but I've heard people may one day live on the Moon, too.

You heard right. A 2015 space study concluded that NASA could begin robotic construction of a permanent base by the year 2021.

These drawings of what a return to the Moon could look like are amazing!

Are there any other places scientists hope to land humans?

NASA is working on that now. If they succeed, they might save the human race from extinction some day!

Why should we worry about extinction?

How else do telescopes figure into the future of space exploration?

In the next 20 years, telescopes will help us look for life on other worlds. The James Webb Space Telescope should launch in 2018. It will orbit the Sun, nearly 1.5 million miles from Earth.

This is cool!

Will it see further and clearer than the Hubble Telescope?

This is another possible future telescope. The Giant Magellan Telescope will collect more light than any telescope in existence.

Yep!

And the ATLAST telescope will be even better!

ATLAST?

Yes — Advanced Technology Large-Aperture Space Telescope. It's set to launch in 2030. It will detect water, gases and other signs of life in distant galaxies.

But regular people won't just experience space through telescope photos. In the future, space tourism might be big business. Space hotels like this one could give tourists all the comforts of Earth.

Maybe someday space tourists could take space walks, just like astronauts!

By the year 2035, space hotels like this might serve dozens of guests a week.

Experts think there could be as many as 500,000 tourists soaring into space each year!

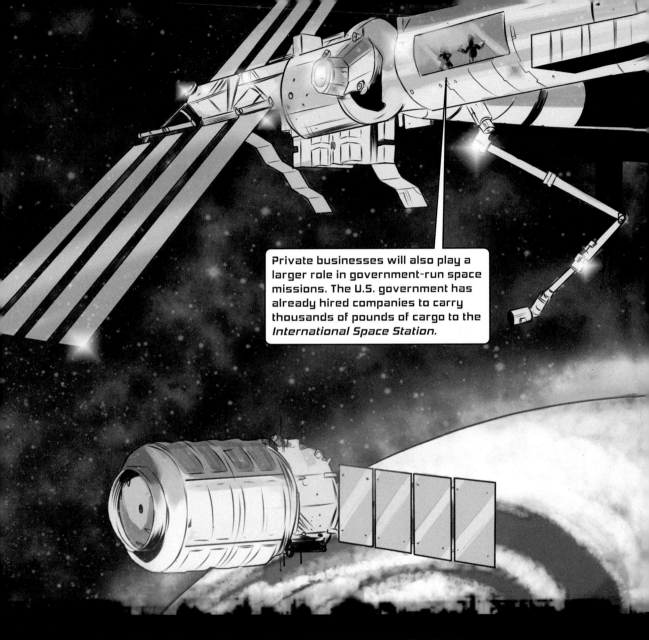

Private businesses will also play a larger role in government-run space missions. The U.S. government has already hired companies to carry thousands of pounds of cargo to the *International Space Station*.

THE HIGH COST OF SPACE TOURISM |||||||||||||||

From 2001 to 2009, eight private citizens each paid £14 million to travel to space aboard missions conducted by the Russian government. By 2014, the private space company Virgin Galactic had sold 700 tickets costing £128,386 each to fly into space aboard the company's rocket plane. The voyage will take passengers about 100 kilometres (62 miles) above Earth. The tickets include three days of space training.

There's an old saying that goes, "It's difficult to make predictions, especially about the future." That's why responsible futurists don't pretend to "predict" the future.

They forecast alternative futures and help people envision and achieve preferred futures.

One forecast sees humans first living on the Moon, and then Mars. Another sees humans going directly to Mars. Humans may avoid planetary living entirely and build free-standing space platforms.

And of course, it's possible that humans will never go to space again. It has been 40 years since humans last visited the Moon. There may be new obstacles to overcome.

Moon settlements will likely be built underground to protect against dangerous forms of radiation.

Wow! That's a lot of work.

The job of establishing a lunar community may start with bringing food, water, machines, building materials and power sources to the Moon.

The Moon doesn't have a protective atmosphere like Earth does. Living underground will help keep homes warmer during the cold nights and cooler during the hot days.

I bet shipping building materials to the Moon will be very expensive.

That's why scientists may want to mine many resources from the Moon itself.

Billions of tons of ice under the Moon's poles could be mined for water. Gases trapped in the lunar surface might provide oxygen to breath. Minerals in lunar rocks may be harvested as sources of energy.

Lunar living could also allow scientists to test new technologies that may help us live on more distant worlds.

In 2012, scientists discovered an Earth-size planet in Alpha Centauri, the star system closest to our own solar system. Some scientists believe planets in Alpha Centauri may be able to support life.

How do we get there?

Reaching Alpha Centauri would take tens of thousands of years with today's spacecraft.

So it's impossible?

Not necessarily. Researchers at NASA are already working on new technologies to help get us there.

And what they've come up with is straight out of a science fiction movie!

Space launches could cost millions, or even billions, of pounds. Each launch to bring supplies and equipment to space stations and future colonies would amount to enormous sums of money.

Space launches require huge amounts of energy to break through Earth's gravitational pull. To solve this problem, some scientists believe a 100,000-kilometre (62,000-mile) space lift could one day carry people and supplies beyond Earth's gravitational pull. From there a launch would use less energy. A space lift could lower the cost of moving 1.6 kilograms (1 pound) of goods into space from £6,000 to about £340.

The heart of the lift is a thin tube-like ribbon made of a carbon substance. The idea is that this flexible ribbon would be 100 times stronger than steel.

How would it get into space?

It would be wound into a ball and launched into orbit. Once there, it would unwind and fall back to Earth.

The ribbon would be anchored to a platform on Earth. Meanwhile, machinery and equipment to power the lift and lift cars will be launched into space. Astronauts could attach it to the ribbon already in orbit.

The equipment at the top of the space lift might even be used to help launch spacecraft to the moons of other planets in our solar system.

I bet NASA has big plans for those moons.

We can find out more on Saturn.

Saturn is the sixth planet from the Sun. And its largest moon, Titan, is one of the most Earth-like worlds scientists have found.

How so?

Titan has rivers, seas and lakes made of liquid methane and ethane. Some scientists believe there may be life in those bodies of liquid.

THE FRONTIER SPIRIT

None of this is certain, Ron. Without the proper support and funding, there may not be a future in space exploration.

I can't wait to see the future of space exploration!

These amazing achievements won't just happen on their own.

What are you saying? That I can affect the future of space travel?

One way or another, you will. Everything you do and every choice you make has an effect on the future. Even doing nothing.

SPACE EXPLORATION

The term "astronaut" comes from the Greek words *stron*, meaning "star," and *nautes*, meaning "sailor."

On July 20, 1969, Neil Armstrong and Edwin "Buzz" Aldrin became the first humans to reach the Moon. Their *Apollo 11* spacecraft touched down in a flat stretch of land named the Sea of Tranquility.

Astronauts who have taken space walks say space smells like fried steak, raspberries, or burning metal.

The 135th and final mission of the U.S. Space Shuttle program was flown in July 2011. It used the Space Shuttle *Atlantis*.

The *International Space Station* weighs about 420 metric tons (925,000 pounds). That's equal to about 320 cars.

The James Webb Space Telescope is NASA's next orbiting space observatory. It will be the successor to the Hubble Space Telescope and is scheduled to launch in October 2018.

You become taller in space. With less gravity pulling down on your body, your spine straightens out. You can become as much as 2 inches (5 cm) taller in space.

In 1970, *Apollo 13* was headed to the Moon when an onboard explosion caused major problems. The astronauts fixed the problems with materials in the craft and returned to Earth safely.

Mars is home to the tallest mountain in our solar system. Olympus Mons, a volcano, is nearly 21 kilometres (69,000 feet) high and 600 kilometres (2 million feet) across! The tallest mountain on Earth is Mount Everest, at 8,850 metres (29,035 feet).

The first woman in space was Russian. Valentine Tereshkova made her historic flight in 1963 on the *Vostock 6* mission. Ms. Tereshkova orbited the Earth 48 times during her nearly 71-hour journey into space.

MORE ABOUT LUNA LI

Futurists are scientists who systematically study and explore possibilities about the future of human society and life on Earth. Luna Li proved herself to be brilliant in this field at a young age. She excelled in STEM subjects and earned her PhD in Alternative Futures from the University of Hawaii at Manoa. Luna invented a gadget she calls the Future Scenario Generator (FSG) that she wears on her wrist. Luna inputs current and predicted data into the FSG. It then crunches the numbers and creates a portal to at holographic reality that humans can enter and interact with.

artificial satellite human-made craft placed in orbit around a planet or moon in order to collect information

asteroid rocky object that travels around the Sun

cosmonaut astronaut from Russia

engineer people who are specially trained to design and build machines or large structures

galaxies very large groups of stars and planets

holograph image made by laser beams that looks as if it has depth and dimension

missile weapon that is aimed at a target

portal doorway or an entrance

radiation tiny particles sent out from radioactive material

rover vehicle used to explore the terrain of a planet or its moons

sediment sand, mud and other particles produced from weathering

How Do Scientists Explore Space? (Earth, Space and Beyond), Robert Snedden (Raintree, 2012)

Space Record Breakers, Anne Rooney (Carlton Kids, 2014)

Who Travelled to the Moon? (Primary Source Detectives), Neil Morris (Raintree, 2014)

The Amazing Story of Space Travel (Graphic Science), Agnieszka Biskup (Raintree, 2014)

WEBSITES

http://www.bbc.com/news/science-environment-35326827
Learn about the most important moments in space exploration.

http://www.bbc.co.uk/education/guides/z496fg8/activity
Learn how stars and galaxies are created.

INDEX